MW01152991

THE KING COBRA

BY LISA OWINGS

BELLWETHER MEDIA • MINNEAPOLIS, MN

Jump into the cockpit and take flight with Pilot Books. Your journey will take you on high-energy adventures as you learn about all that is wild, weird, fascinating, and fun!

This edition first published in 2012 by Bellwether Media, Inc.

Library of Congress Cataloging-in-Publication Data

Owings, Lisa.
The king cobra / by Lisa Owings.
p. cm. – (Pilot books. Nature's deadliest)
Includes bibliographical references and index.
Summary: "Fascinating images accompany information about the king cobra. The combination of high-interest subject matter and narrative text is intended for students in grades 3 through 7"–Provided by publisher.
ISBN 978-1-60014-743-2 (hardcover : alk. paper)
1. King cobra–Juvenile literature. I. Title.
QL666.O64O95 2012
597.96'42–dc23 2011036521

Printed in the United States of America, North Mankato, MN.

010112 1204

CONTENTS

The Few Survivors

Bill Haast was the first person known to survive a king cobra bite. After a lifelong fascination with snakes, he opened the Miami **Serpentarium** in 1946. His main goal was to collect snake **venom** for medicine. Haast had already been bitten by many venomous snakes when he started **injecting** himself with venom. This helped him develop **immunity** to the deadly poison. Still, his body was unprepared for one terrifying day in 1962.

Haast was handling one of the deadliest snakes of all, the king cobra. He made one wrong move, and the lightning-fast snake sank its fangs into his hand. Haast arrived at the hospital with mild swelling around the bite. All of a sudden, his body shut down and his heart stopped. Doctors gave him **antivenom** and **adrenaline** to get his heart pumping again. After a few hours, Haast felt well enough to leave the hospital. He went right back to harvesting venom.

The second person known to survive a king cobra bite was Robert Hughes. Like Haast, Hughes was passionate about venomous snakes. In 1982, he was inspecting a shipment of king cobras from Thailand when something went very wrong. Hughes felt fangs pierce his thumb.

Unlike Haast, Hughes had no immunity. At first, he felt a rush of warmth. Then his vision began to blur. Colors faded to black and white. He felt intense pain, and he couldn't move or speak. When he arrived at the hospital an hour later, he was unconscious. He needed a machine to help him breathe. Doctors pumped fifty **vials** of antivenom through his veins. Against all odds, Hughes recovered a few days later.

Making Antivenom

A small amount of snake venom is injected into an animal, usually a horse. The animal's immune system fights the venom by producing antibodies. These are proteins that stop the venom from doing harm. The antibodies are collected and made into antivenom.

Bill Haast played a role in Hughes' survival. The venom he harvested helped make antivenom, which is what saved Hughes and many others. Haast risked his life every day to collect venom. He made the deadliest snakes in the world angry enough to produce venom. He used one hand to distract the snake and grabbed its head with the other. Then he put the snake's fangs over a glass vial where the venom was collected.

In this dangerous line of work, Haast was bitten more than 170 times. Throughout his career, he injected himself with a mixture of snake venoms. This allowed him to survive each near-fatal bite, including at least two king cobra bites. Haast lived to be 100 years old!

One Man Blood Bank

Bill Haast's blood contained valuable antibodies due to his venom injections. He saved at least 21 lives by flying around the world to donate his blood to snakebite victims.

A Venomous King

The king cobra is the largest venomous snake on Earth. It is found in India and much of Southeast Asia. It can grow to be more than 18 feet (5.5 meters) long. When ready to **strike**, it can raise a third of its body off the ground. That means a large king cobra can look you in the face before it attacks.

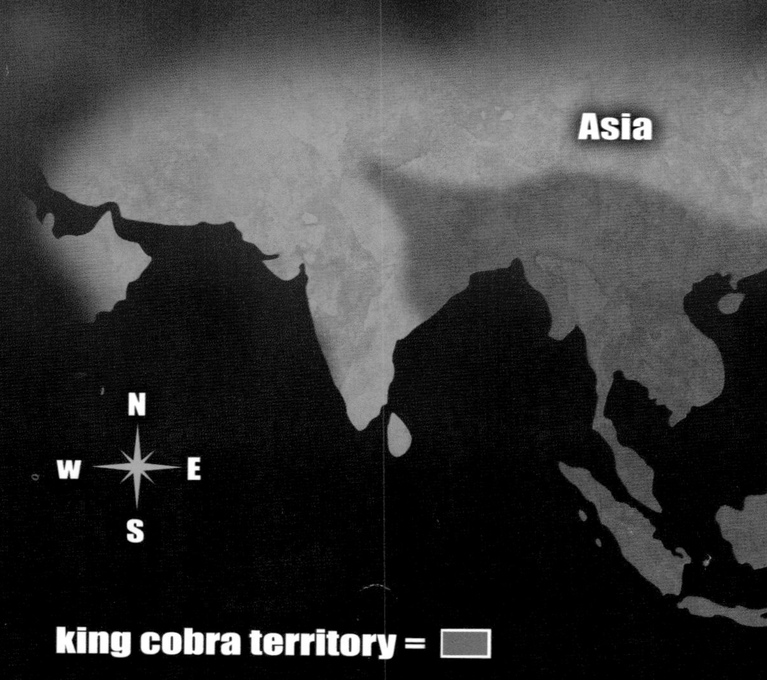

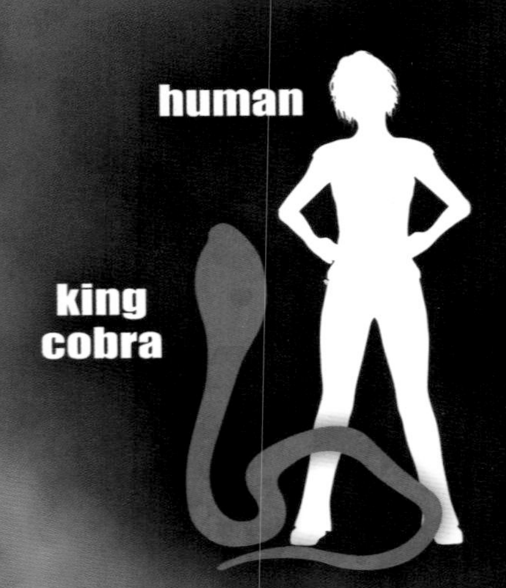

The king cobra is similar to other cobras. Cobras are venomous snakes that can spread the skin around their necks into a **hood**. It can be hard to distinguish a king cobra from a cobra, but there are differences. The king cobra has arrow-shaped markings instead of the circular markings most cobras have. It also has larger scales on its head.

The king cobra does not have the most powerful venom of any snake. However, one bite from a king cobra can deliver up to 1.5 teaspoons (7 milliliters) of venom. That is more than any other snake. It is enough to kill 20 adult humans, or one fully grown elephant.

King cobras have short, hollow, needle-sharp fangs. Unlike most other snakes, the fangs of a king cobra are **fixed**. This means they are always set forward and ready to inject venom. King cobra venom causes severe pain and **paralysis**. It quickly stops the heart and lungs. Most victims die within an hour.

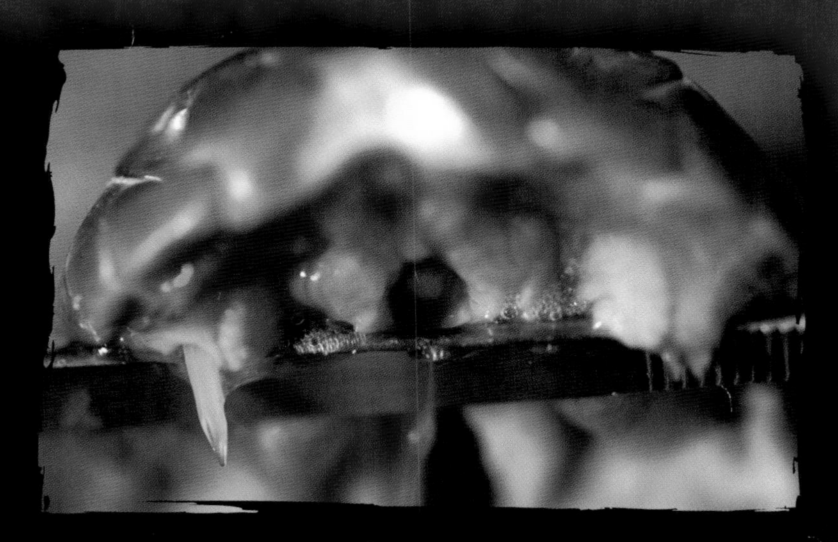

Sudden Death

King cobra venom can kill a human in less than fifteen minutes.

Nowhere to Hide

King cobras live in jungles near rivers and lakes. They are skilled swimmers and can also climb trees!

King cobras are stealthy hunters that eat mostly other snakes. The king cobra hunts during the day. It slithers through tall grasses looking for a meal. To catch the scent of prey, it flicks its tongue in and out. It silently sneaks up on its chosen victim. Then it raises the front part of its body off the ground. Its hooded head sways back and forth.

The king cobra strikes quickly. The other snake struggles for a few minutes, then dies. The king cobra swallows its prey whole, inch by inch. A king cobra may not need to eat for months after a large meal.

Keen Senses

Like other snakes, the king cobra can sense vibrations through the ground when other animals are near. It can also sense the heat of other animals.

King Cobra Attacks

King cobras usually save their venom for prey. They do not attack humans except in life-threatening situations. King cobras generally attack people only when trapped. Before biting, they warn people with a low hiss that sounds like a dog's growl.

King cobras are very protective of their young. They are the only snakes that make nests and guard their eggs. If a person or animal approaches its nest, the king cobra will attack.

King Cobra vs. Mongoose

Mongooses are brave little animals that have a resistance to cobra venom. They are also quick enough to dodge a cobra's strike. Mongooses sometimes attack king cobras. However, the king cobra is large, dangerous, and not afraid to fight back. Mongooses usually go after easier prey.

People in Southeast Asia do everything they can to avoid a king cobra bite. They know where king cobras are most active and avoid those places when possible. They travel in groups when entering king cobra **habitat**. They also move slowly and wear shoes and long pants.

If a king cobra is spotted, people are careful not to come within striking distance. This is usually about one-third the length of the king cobra's body. If a cobra hisses or stands and displays its hood, people back away. They know never to corner a king cobra.

King Cobra Bite First Aid

It is important to act quickly when treating a king cobra bite. After you send someone to get help, wash the bite wound with soap and water. Wrap elastic bandages around the bitten limb to help keep the venom from spreading. Try to keep the victim still and the bite wound lower than the heart.

Charming Snakes

King cobras are popular with snake charmers. They cannot hear the music of the charmer's flute. Rather, they see the instrument as a threat and match its movements.

Attack Facts

- **Fewer than five humans are killed each year by king cobras.**
- **Most antivenom is made in Thailand and India, where most king cobra attacks occur.**

People all over the world are fascinated by the deadly king cobra. However, the king cobra is in danger of going **extinct**. Many people hunt the king cobra to harvest its venom for medicine. Others hunt king cobras for their skin or meat. Snake charmers in India catch them to use in their shows. The number of king cobras in the wild has fallen considerably over the past 75 years. Many people are working hard to save king cobras in order to learn more about them. It is possible to appreciate their power and avoid their deadly bite!

Glossary

adrenaline—a chemical the body produces when it needs more energy or senses danger

antivenom—a substance used to treat venomous bites

extinct—no longer existing as a species

fixed—unable to be moved; a king cobra's fangs do not fold back like those of most other snakes.

habitat—the environment in which a plant or animal usually lives

hood—the spread-out neck skin of a king cobra

immunity—protection from harm or sickness

injecting—putting fluid into the body through a sharp point; a king cobra injects venom through its fangs.

paralysis—loss of the ability to move or feel

serpentarium—a museum or zoo specializing in snakes

strike—to attack suddenly and forcefully; a king cobra strikes with a quick, downward motion.

venom—poison produced by snakes and some other animals; a king cobra delivers more venom per bite than any other snake.

vials—small glass containers, usually for liquids

To Learn More

At the Library

Graham, Audry. *King Cobra*. New York, N.Y.: Gareth Stevens Pub., 2011.

Mattern, Joanne. *King Cobras*. Mankato, Minn.: Capstone Press, 2010.

White, Nancy. *King Cobras: The Biggest Venomous Snakes of All!* New York, N.Y.: Bearport Pub., 2009.

On the Web

Learning more about king cobras is as easy as 1, 2, 3.

1. Go to www.factsurfer.com.

2. Enter "king cobras" into the search box.

3. Click the "Surf" button and you will see a list of related Web sites.

With factsurfer.com, finding more information is just a click away.

Index

The images in this book are reproduced through the courtesy of: Henry Wilson, front cover; Dave Stamboulis Travel Photography / Getty Images, p. 5; Heiko Kiera, p. 6; Mattias Klum / National Geographic Stock, pp. 8, 12 (small), 13; Fox Photos / Getty Images, p. 9; Matthew Cole, p. 11; Biosphoto / Olivier Born / Biosphoto, pp. 14-15; Daniel Heuclin / Photolibrary, p. 16; Mark O'Shea / Photoshot, p. 17; Biosphoto / Olivier Born / Biosphoto, p. 18; Dan Saunders Photography / Alamy, p. 20.